STARTING OUT

I0896008

baby KITTIES

LAURA K. MURRAY

CREATIVE EDUCATION • CREATIVE PAPERBACKS

CONT

ENTS

I AM A KITTEN.

I am a baby cat.

Look at my long tail and pointed ears!

I am tiny at birth. I can fit in a person's hand! My eyes and ears are closed for the first few weeks.

I crawl and wiggle. I meow when I am hungry. My mother feeds me milk.

Whiskers grow on my face

They help me sense the world around me. My whiskers should not be cut.

I run, play, and explore after five weeks!

I eat wet or
dry food.
I lick my fur to
clean it.

I use a litter box. At nine months, my teeth grow in. I eat adult cat food and sleep a lot.

Come play with me!

SPEAK AND LISTEN

MEE

oooow!

Can you speak like a kitten? Cats can meow, hiss, and purr.

Listen to these sounds:

Now it is your turn!

KITTEN WORDS

litter box: a box or tray with dry material where a cat can go to the bathroom

sense: to gather information about the area

whisker: a thin, stiff hair on an animal's face

READING CORNER

Greenwood, Nancy. *My Pet Cat*. New York: Gareth Stevens, 2023.

Leaf, Christina. *Baby Cat or Baby Dog?* Minneapolis: Bellwether Media, 2024.

Rossiter, Brienna. *My Pet Cat*. Mendota Heights, Minn.: Little Blue House, 2022.

INDEX

PUBLISHED BY CREATIVE EDUCATION AND CREATIVE PAPERBACKS
P.O. Box 227, Mankato, Minnesota 56002
Creative Education and Creative Paperbacks are imprints of The Creative Company
www.thecreativecompany.us

LIBRARY OF CONGRESS CATALOGING-IN-PUBLICATION DATA
Names: Murray, Laura K., ‡d 1989- author
Title: Baby kitties / by Laura K. Murray.
Other titles: Baby kittens
Description: Mankato, Minnesota : Creative Education and Creative Paperbacks, [2026] | Series: Starting out | Includes bibliographical references and index. | Audience: Ages 4-7 | Audience: Grades K-1 | Summary: "Introduce beginning readers to the world of baby kitties with this life science starter. Includes photos, a labeled animal diagram, "Speak and Listen" section, glossary, and further resources"— Provided by publisher.
Identifiers: LCCN 2025015274 (print) | LCCN 2025015275 (ebook) | ISBN 9798895810347 library binding | ISBN 9781682779873 paperback | ISBN 9798895811603 ebook
Subjects: LCSH: Kittens--Juvenile literature | Kittens--Behavior--Miscellanea--Juvenile literature
Classification: LCC SF445.7 .M867 2026 (print) | LCC SF445.7 (ebook) | DDC 636.8/07--dc23/eng/20250717
LC record available at https://lccn.loc.gov/2025015274
LC ebook record available at https://lccn.loc.gov/2025015275

DESIGN AND PRODUCTION
Design by Rhea Magaro
Art direction by Tom Morgan

PHOTOGRAPHS BY
Dreamstime/Denys Prokofyev, 2, Isselee, 11, Marazem, 10, S-dmit, 7, Tony Campbell, 12; Getty Images/Paul Biris, 8; Shutterstock/Oleksandr Lytvynenko, cover; Unsplash/claudia perez, 6, Ivan Nee, 5, Road Ahead, 9, The Lucky Neko, 14; Wikimedia Commons/kitty.green66, 4

Printed in the United States